Everything You Need To Know About

SEXUAL ABUSE

Boys and girls should be told how to protect themselves from sexual abuse.

• THE NEED TO KNOW LIBRARY •

Everything You Need To Know About

SEXUAL ABUSE

Evan Stark, Ph.D.

and

Marsha Holly, Ph.D.

THE ROSEN PUBLISHING GROUP, INC.

NEW YORK

Published in 1988, 1991, 1993 by The Rosen Publishing Group, Inc.
29 East 21st Street, New York, New York 10010

Revised Edition 1993
Copyright © 1988, 1991, 1993 by The Rosen Publishing Group, Inc.

Manufactured in the United States of America.

Library of Congress Cataloging-in-Publication Data

Stark, Evan.
    Everything you need to know about sexual abuse / Evan Stark and
Marsha Holly.
    (The need to know library)
    Includes bibliographical references and index.
    Summary: Identifies forms of sexual abuse and offers advice on how
to get help and how to avoid such abuse.
    ISBN 0-8239-1611-1
    1. Child molesting—juvenile literature. 2. Incest—juvenile literature.
[1. Child molesting. 2. Incest. 3. Child abuse.] I. Holly, Marsha. II. Title.
III. Series.
HQ71.S72 1988
362.7'044—dc19   88-18114
                                                CIP
                                                AC

Contents

Introduction

All of us want to be loved. When people love us, they often show it by hugging, kissing, or touching us. This makes us feel good—as long as they are gentle and respect us.

But when the hugs hurt or the touching turns rough, beware. This may not be love. It may be abuse. When this happens, it's time to get help.

Abusing means using something in a wrong way. A person who sexually abuses someone uses kissing, hugging, or sexual contact in a bad way.

Sexual abusers treat their victims cruelly. They hurt their bodies, their minds, or both. An abuser may hurt your body by forcing you down on the ground and lying on top of you. An abuser may squeeze you or pinch you so hard that it hurts. An abuser may hurt your mind by promising you something you really want and then never giving it to you. An abuser may force you to perform a sexual act that will make you ashamed and depressed for the rest of your life.

Sexual abuse happens most often to children. Sometimes the abuser is a stranger. But more often

All children like to be touched by someone they love and trust.

he or she is a relative, a family friend, or an adult who is respected in the community—someone the child knows. The abuser can even be another child.

The thought of sexual abuse is frightening. But by knowing more about it, you may be able to help yourself, a friend, or a family member who is suffering. Stopping sexual abuse is not your responsibility. It is up to adults to stop it. But understanding some of the warning signs *is* your responsibility. When you understand more about it, you will be better able to help.

An invitation may not feel right. It's best to say "no."

Chapter 1

Just Say No

The Friendly Stranger

You are waiting for the school bus with some friends. A car pulls up. A man leans out, smiles, and calls you over. He asks where the nearest Happy Burger is. You tell him.

"Do you want to come along?" he asks.

You'd love to go to Happy Burger. But you say no. When he leaves, you and your friends talk about it. They agree you did the right thing. "He was weird," a friend says.

The rules about strangers are clear. If the man got out of the car and tried to grab you, you would be scared. But you would know what to say and do. You would tell the man to get lost. You might scream, call for help, kick him, pull away, or run. When you got home, you would tell your parents. They might call the police.

The Strange Friend

This time, you know the man in the car. He's the coach from your school.

"Do you want a ride?" the coach asks.

You're not sure what to do. Your friends are watching. You feel funny. You don't want to be rude.

"Go ahead," says a friend. You get in the car.

On the way home he stops at Happy Burger. He gets you a Coke and a burger, to go. As you're leaving, he pats your backside. You feel funny again. Is something wrong?

When you return to the car, he puts his arm around you. His arm feels safe. But you pull away. He takes his arm away. Then he puts his hand on your leg. He stops at the edge of the park. He asks if you feel lonely. While you talk, he rubs your leg. He rubs your leg in a way that makes you feel uncomfortable.

He takes you to your house. "See you," he says.

Later, your mother asks about your day. You tell her about the ride home. But you don't tell her that the coach rubbed your leg and patted your backside. You act so strange that she asks what's wrong. After dinner, you cry. Then you tell her what happened. Talking makes you feel better.

Abusers Are Often People You Trust

When you were young, you were warned about strangers who try to grab or hurt young people. Those persons are called *molesters*. Molesters are almost always men. And they are usually strangers.

But did you know that people your age are much more likely to be hurt or bothered sexually by a person they know well, like the coach? It could be a scout leader, a neighbor, a doctor, a teacher, a minister, or the father of a friend. Or it could be a member of your own family, like your brother, father, or stepfather. The family members who most often abuse children are fathers and brothers. Sometimes even mothers abuse their children.

We are taught to respect and obey older persons. The hardest thing about sexual abuse is that the abuser is usually someone you trust. It may be someone who is responsible for taking care of you. It may be someone you love. It is almost always someone you want to care about you. The problem is that you may not know how to act or what to say when this happens.

Do you have the right to ask your big brother or sister to knock on the bedroom door before they enter the room?

Can you tell your mom or dad they can't come in the bathroom if you don't want them there?

What happens if your babysitter says "I will let you stay up late and watch a video if you play a game with me and take off your clothes?"

The first step in dealing with sexual abuse is learning how to say no. The problem is that saying no to an adult or someone you trust is not always easy. That's why you have this book.

Teachers and parents help youngsters by listening and talking about sexual abuse.

Chapter 2

What Is Sexual Abuse?

T his chapter answers questions that are often asked about sexual abuse.

What do we mean by "sexual?"

"Sexual" means the parts of your body that can give you great pleasure when you are in love. The main sexual parts of the body are a girl's vagina and a boy's penis. These body organs are used in reproduction and are called *genitals*. In the story, the coach rubbed the young person's leg in a sexual way. Other parts of your body such as your breasts, your backside, or your mouth can also be sexual.

Sexual abuse means using a child for sexual pleasure. Sexual abuse is a crime.

Sexual abuse usually happens only on the sexual parts of the body. Many dads have kissed a little girl's toes, fingertips, knees, tummy, and backside. But when those kisses or rubs are *only* on the tummy, backside, or chest—even if they aren't on the genitals—they probably are bad.

The abuser may touch a young person's sexual parts. The abuser may want the child to touch him (or her) sexually. Or the abuser may use the young person in some other way for sexual activity.

A male may put his penis into a girl's vagina. This is called *intercourse*. A female abuser may force a young boy to have intercourse. When a child has intercourse with a parent, a brother, or a sister, the abuse is called *incest*. Pregnancy is one danger when abuse includes intercourse.

Who are the victims of sexual abuse?

What do you think? Was the child in the two stories a boy or a girl?

You probably said girl. Girls are more likely to be abused than boys. The child in the story could also have been a boy. Boys are also sexually abused. Whether the victim is a boy or a girl, most sexual abuse is committed by men. But women can also commit sexual abuse.

Children are most in danger of being sexually abused when they are between the ages of nine and twelve years old. But a child of two, or a young adult of seventeen could become a victim of abuse.

How common is sexual abuse?

Sexual abuse is far more common than most people think. So is incest.

Count the girls and boys in your class. Do you think any children in your class had an experience like the child in the story? Some may have. One out of every four girls and one out of every six boys may be sexually abused before they reach eighteen.

Are sexual abusers violent?

Many abusers use force. Others use threats. The abuser may threaten to hurt the child or someone the child loves, like her mother. Or a parent may threaten to go away and never come back if the child tells what happened. Or he may say that the child will be taken away if anyone learns about the abuse.

But sexual abuse does not always involve force or threats. Many abusers use bribes or presents to get the child to do what they want. They promise something special, like money or new clothes.

Often sexual abuse starts with a game, like tickling or grabbing or make-believe. The abuser wants the child to trust him. Then, one day, the game becomes sexual.

Does sexual abuse always hurt?

Sexual abuse can cause serious problems even when there is no violence or intercourse. Children

who are abused feel isolated from other children.
They may feel ashamed about what has happened.
They may think they are not worth much. Those
feelings are called low self-esteem. They may feel
so angry that they hurt another child, or a pet. Or
they may try to hurt themselves. Some children
who are sexually abused become very sad or
withdrawn. This is called depression.

Sexual abuse can also cause problems when a
child becomes an adult. Adults who were sexually
abused often don't trust others. Or they may want
to avoid sex altogether.

The longer sexual abuse goes on, the more
damage it can cause.

Not all children who are sexually abused suffer
long-term effects. If the abuse is stopped early and
the child finds someone they trust to talk to, many
of the harmful effects of sexual abuse can be
prevented.

Who commits sexual abuse?

A myth is something most people believe that is
not true. One myth is that sexual abusers are sick.
Another myth is that sexual abuse only happens in
families that have a lot of other problems as well.

Some abusers have serious mental health
problems. Some are sexually attracted to children,
but not to other adults. And some abusers were
sexually or physically abused themselves when they
were children. Some families where sexual abuse

Finding a friend to talk to can help stop abuse.

occurs also have other problems. The husband may be beating his wife. The mother may be disabled.

But most sexual abuse occurs in ordinary families and is committed by ordinary men.

The abuser wants things his own way. He likes being in control and having power over others. This is why he is attracted to someone who is smaller and weaker than he is, like a child.

How have we learned so much about sexual abuse?

We learn about sexual abuse when people who have been sexually abused tell their stories.

Adults who were hurt by sexual abuse as children are talking about it. Children are talking too. They are telling their stories to teachers, nurses, parents, and friends—to anyone who will listen.

Parents, doctors, teachers, police, and others who want to help and protect children are learning about sexual abuse.

Sexual abuse is on TV and the radio and in the newspapers. Young people all over are speaking out. Sexual abuse is the secret that is now being shared.

Chapter 3

Rules to Remember About Sexual Abuse

The stories in this book come from girls and boys who got help. The boys and girls use seven rules to solve their problems. These rules can help you understand and respond to sexual abuse.

Rule #1. YOUR BODY BELONGS TO YOU.
You, and only you, should decide how to use your body sexually. In sexual abuse, someone who is older and more powerful decides how to use your body. This is wrong. You have a right to say no.

Rule #2. SEXUAL ABUSE IS NEVER YOUR FAULT.
Children are not responsible for what adults or other older persons do. Abuse is not their fault, even if they cannot say no or if they enjoy the attention they get from the abuser. Nothing a child does, or doesn't do, excuses an older person who uses a child for sexual pleasure.

Some men attend counseling sessions to discuss their problems as abusers.

Rule #3. SEXUAL ABUSE IS ALWAYS HARMFUL.

Sexual abuse always hurts the child. Sometimes the child's body is hurt. If a girl who is old enough to have babies is abused, she can get pregnant. But the deepest hurt is the way sexual abuse makes children feel. Sexual abuse always makes children feel bad about themselves. These feelings can make it hard to work in school, to have friends, or to have fun.

Rule #4. GOOD PEOPLE CAN DO BAD THINGS.

It is hard to believe that someone we love or who is kind to us can sexually abuse us. Abusers may be good persons in other ways. They may give presents. Or they may be gentle when they want sex. But the abuse is very, very wrong and must be stopped.

Rule #5. SEXUAL ABUSE DOES NOT STOP BY ITSELF.

Sexual abuse is hard to talk about. Children are sometimes afraid of the abuser. But sexual abuse usually goes on until the abuser is made to stop. The best way to stop sexual abuse is to tell an adult who will listen and do something about it.

There are special people, child workers, whose job is to protect children from abuse. Adults know how to find these people.

Sexual abuse always hurts. It creates feelings of shame and loneliness.

Rule #6. <u>KEEP TELLING PEOPLE YOU
    TRUST ABOUT SEXUAL ABUSE UNTIL
    SOMEONE LISTENS.</u>
Some adults may not believe a child. Other
adults may tell the young person to forget about
the problem. But remember, sexual abuse does not
stop by itself. If one adult doesn't do the right
thing, tell another who will.

Rule #7. <u>WHAT HAPPENS TO A SEXUAL
    ABUSER IS NEVER YOUR FAULT.</u>
Children feel, "If I tell, then what happens to
the abuser is my fault." Because sexual abuse is a
crime, some abusers go to jail. Others leave the
house. When the abuser is someone you care
about, this is very hard. Some abusers stop when
they are told it is wrong. Some abusers need to see
a doctor. Remember, only the sexual abuser is
responsible for what happens when abuse is
uncovered.

The next few chapters tell the stories of children
who said no to abuse. See if the Seven Rules help
you understand what happened to them—and what
they did *to help themselves*.

Chapter 4

Good People Can Do Bad Things

Debra lives in a house with her mom, her dad, her grandfather and her dog. After her eleventh birthday party, she looked at herself in the mirror. She noticed that her breasts were beginning to form.

Sexual Abusers Can Be Family Members

Suddenly, Debra's grandfather walked into the room. He laughed at her in front of the mirror. He made fun of her body.

"I suppose you think you need a bra," he teased.

Debra felt hurt. She had wondered if she could wear a bra. Some of her friends wore them already. But what her grandfather said made her feel ashamed. When he made fun of her, she thought she was no good.

A few weeks later, her grandfather walked into the bathroom while Debra was taking a bath. At first

A father should respect his daughter's privacy.

she thought it was a mistake. But he wouldn't leave when she asked him. She wrapped a towel around herself. But he yanked it off. Then he grabbed her from behind. He held her breasts.

"Cut it out," she yelled. She tried to get free.

"You used to like being tickled," he said.

"I'm not a little girl anymore," Debra said. She got really angry. She felt dirty and wanted to die. He told her not to tell her parents or he would have to leave the house.

She didn't want her grandfather to go. Although he kept bothering her, she decided not to tell her mom and dad.

Debra is growing up. Her body is changing. She feels bashful because she is not always sure what's happening. She needs time to get used to her body. It's really a new body all the time. Debra needs privacy to explore herself and learn about her body. She has a right to privacy. Some day she will want someone her own age to touch her breasts. And that's okay.

Her grandfather has no respect for Debra. He wants to see her naked. He pretends he's kidding. But abuse is no joke.

Tell Someone You Trust

One day, Mrs. Markle, a teacher at Debra's school, saw her crying in the girl's bathroom. Debra told Mrs. Markle why she was so upset. Mrs. Markle questioned Debra closely. Then she told

Debra she had done the right thing to tell her. She explained that there was no reason for Debra to hate herself. The feelings she has about herself come from her grandfather's abuse.

Mrs. Markle called a social worker at the child protection office and the social worker came to the house. She explained that Debra's grandpa would have to live somewhere else.

When Debra got home, her mother was angry. "Why didn't you just tell me what happened?" she yelled.

"I didn't think you would believe me," Debra said. "And grandpa told me not to tell or he would have to leave the house."

"I don't want grandpa to go either but he'll have to." her mother said. "I'm really upset you didn't tell me. I would have stopped him."

Remembering the Rules

The most important lesson Debra learned was Rule #1, Your Body Belongs to You.

It's *your* body. You have a right to have your body respected, comforted, and loved only in ways that please you or that benefit you.

Rule #2, Abuse Is Never Your Fault.

Nothing Debra did was wrong. Children are not responsible for the sexual behavior of adults.

Rule #4, Good People Do Bad Things.

Debra's grandfather may be good in other ways. But his abuse is wrong and must be stopped.

Finding someone who will listen is the first step toward ending abuse.

Community Leaders Can Be Abusers

Debra's abuser was a family member. Chris and Ronnie were sexually abused by one of the most respected people in town—the Catholic priest. Chris' abuse started when he was 17; Ronnie was 13. Both came from homes without fathers. They needed the love and respect of an older man, someone who would be like a father to them. The priest took advantage of that need.

Ronnie is older now, but he is deeply troubled by his past. He has had serious thoughts of suicide.

Chris and Ronnie didn't know each other. For a long time, neither said anything to anyone. They were afraid of what might happen to themselves and to the priest. Both wanted to believe that this man did love them. They didn't want to admit they were being abused.

It's hard to believe that people we love and respect can treat us cruelly. But it does happen sometimes. Even people who are well-known and loved by your community—religious leaders, counselors, politicians, and school administrators— can betray a trust and become abusers. When and if that occurs, we must admit what is happening and get help right away.

This does not mean that you should become suspicious of all adults. Most people are good. It means that you should recognize sexual abuse when you see or hear about it. Keep in mind Rule #4, Good People Can Do Bad Things.

Chapter 5

Sexual Abuse Is Never Your Fault

Leota is almost nine. She lives with her mother and her seventeen-year-old brother, Alonzo. They live in a two-room apartment. She and Alonzo share a room. Sometimes her mother works at night. When this happens, Alonzo baby-sits. When Leota goes to bed, Alonzo stays up to watch TV.

Leota's friends think Alonzo is a great dancer. Leota wishes Alonzo would pay attention to her. When she tries to get his attention, he tells her to shut up or go away.

Leota's Brother Is an Abuser

The first time Alonzo bothered Leota in bed, she was almost asleep. She felt hands on her bottom. She thought it was her mother tucking her in. The next night she heard Alonzo cross the room. He sat

Sexual abuse can destroy the trust between a brother and sister.

on the edge of her bed. He put his hand in her pajamas. He felt around below her tummy. Then he went back to his bed. She lay awake and felt scared.

A week later her brother touched her again. This time she pretended to be asleep. He put his hand in her pajamas and started rubbing her genitals. When this happened she had a tingling feeling. She was also confused. She wanted Alonzo to like her. She knew that what he was doing was wrong. But she thought it was her fault.

Alonzo continued to sexually abuse Leota. When Alonzo rubbed her, neither of them spoke. Several times he even got under the covers with Leota. Then he rubbed his penis against her. She kept her eyes closed. Outside the bedroom Alonzo pretended Leota didn't exist.

Leota started to worry all the time. She felt different from her friends. She stayed by herself. She was sure everyone knew about her and Alonzo. She had trouble in school. She failed tests in spelling, her best subject.

One day Maria, a girl in Leota's class, asked what was wrong. Leota told her. Maria listened

Leota started to worry all the time. She felt different from her friends. She stayed by herself.

carefully. She didn't fully understand. But she knew Alonzo was hurting Leota. The next day Maria's mother called Leota's mother on the phone. They talked for a long time.

That night Leota's mother stayed home from work. She made Alonzo move his bed into the living room. She moved her own bed into the room with Leota. The next time she had to work at night she called Carmen, Maria's older sister, to baby-sit for Leota.

Leota's mother called a child worker. The child worker made Alonzo go to a doctor about his problem.

For several weeks Leota blushed whenever she saw Alonzo. Then she felt okay. She and Maria became best friends.

A year later, Alonzo told Leota he was sorry about what he had done.

Remembering the Rules

The most important lesson Leota learned was Rule #2, Sexual Abuse Is Never Your Fault.

Leota knew that Alonzo liked to touch her. She loved her brother. She wanted him to hug her and love her back. She thought he would love her more if she let him do what he wanted.

Children want and need affection. Sometimes older people make it hard to get affection in good

Constant worrying may lead to depression.

ways. Children sometimes think they have to get it any way they can. But no matter how a child acts, she or he should not be abused.

Leota lay in her bed quietly when Alonzo touched her. Does that mean what happened was her fault? No. The victim of sexual abuse is never to blame. Children simply are not responsible for what an older, stronger person does.

Rule #5 is Sexual Abuse Does Not Stop by Itself.

Maria saw something was wrong. She asked to help. This was very brave. But Maria could not stop Alonzo. So she told her mother. When Alonzo's mother found out, she called a child worker. A child worker's job is to protect children from abuse. Alonzo would not have stopped bothering his sister if Maria had not told her mother.

Rule #7 is What Happens to the Abuser Is Never Your Fault.

Alonzo's bed was moved. He had to go for help. All this was his fault, not Leota's. Still, Leota felt sorry for Alonzo.

The Oprah Winfrey Story

Many famous people have suffered sexual abuse. Talk-show host Oprah Winfrey is one of them. When she was 9, she was raped by her 19-year-old cousin. From then until she was 14, she was sexually abused by a friend of the family. A favorite uncle also molested her. "You lose your childhood when you've been abused," says Oprah.

At last, when she was 14, Oprah went to live with her father, Vernon. Only then did the abuse stop. But a great deal of damage had already been done. For years the famous TV star lived a tortured life because of her past. She felt guilty and ashamed. It took Oprah a long time to realize Rule #2 about sexual abuse: Sexual Abuse Is Never

Sometimes older people make it hard to get affection in good ways.

Your Fault. "The truth is, the child is never to blame," Oprah now admits. "It took me 37 years to figure that out."

One night Oprah heard a news report that a 4-year-old Chicago girl had been abused, strangled, and thrown into a lake. "I vowed that night to do something, to take a stand for the children of this country," she said. Today Oprah Winfrey is using her popularity and her television show to help other young victims of sexual abuse.

Oprah suggested an idea for a new law. The law would require that a list be kept of all people convicted of child abuse and other similar crimes. When a person applied for a job working with children, such as at a school, day care center, or camp, the person's name would be checked against this list. Six states already have this law, but Oprah wants all states to have it.

"We have to [show] that we value our children," she believes. So she's also working on a plan to have the law punish every child molester. "These people must know," she says, "that when you hurt a child, this is what happens to you."

Oprah Winfrey learned Rule #5 the hard way: Sexual Abuse Does Not Stop By Itself. She knows that in order to make it stop, people must take action.

Abused children sometimes become bullies.

Chapter 6

Boys Are Victims, Too

Billy was eleven years old. A seven-year-old boy named Sam lived next door. Sam had a rabbit named Black Jack. Sam loved Black Jack very much.

One day the boys were alone in Billy's yard. Billy told Sam to follow him into the garage. "I have something special for you," Billy said. Billy closed the door. He unzipped his pants and took out his penis. He grabbed Sam by the neck and pushed him down.

"Put it in your mouth," he told Sam. "If you don't, I'll kill Black Jack." Sam did what Billy said.

Billy told Sam his father and mother would die if he told. "And I won't be your friend," Billy said. Sam was very scared. So he kept the secret.

Sam was in the first grade. At school he started hitting other children. The teacher asked Sam's parents if anything was wrong. She also asked Sam. But he kept quiet.

Things got worse. Sam started to wet his bed. He woke up in the night crying. His mother went to his bed. Sam said, "I don't want you to die, Mommy."

One day Sam was in the bathroom at school with another little boy. They had their pants down. Sam grabbed the boy. He pointed to his penis. "Take it in your mouth," he said. The boy knocked Sam down, and Sam cried. Then Sam told the teacher what Billy had made him do in the garage. The teacher was very upset. She told Sam's parents. She also called a child worker.

Sam's father yelled at Billy. Later he yelled at Billy's mother. Billy started to cry. He told his mother that a bigger boy had been making him do the same thing he made Sam do. The bigger boy was a bully. Billy was afraid of him, just as Sam was afraid of Billy.

The child worker went to Sam's house. First she talked to Sam, then to Billy. She also visited the bully and his family. The bully was sent for help.

Remembering the Rules

The most important lesson to learn from this story is Rule #3, Sexual Abuse Is Always Harmful.

Sometimes children who are sexually abused will abuse other children who are weaker. Or they may hurt pets. When Billy was abused, he didn't know what to do. He was scared. But he was also angry. He felt that this should not have happened to a big boy like him. Maybe something was wrong with him, he thought. He felt bad about himself. He didn't want anyone to find out that he was weak. So he proved he was stronger than Sam. He abused his friend.

When a Boy Is Sexually Abused

In our society, boys and men are expected to be tough. If you cry, people may say you're a sissy. If you can't protect yourself, people may say you're a wimp. Of course this thinking is silly. But it's one reason why 9 out of 10 cases of sexual abuse never get reported when males are the victims.

The truth is that one out of every six boys will probably suffer some kind of sexual abuse before he is 18. Many times the victims are boys who have no fathers at home or whose fathers show no love for them. The abuser is often someone the boy knows, a family friend or relative.

Some boys are afraid that being abused by a man makes them *homosexual*. A homosexual is a person who has sexual feelings toward people of the same sex. This keeps many male victims silent about the abuse. But boys as well as girls, remember, if you have been sexually abused, Speak Up!

Two sisters share the hurt of their father's sexual abuse.

Chapter 7

The Problem of Incest

Roseann was twelve. She and her older sister, Doreen, lived in a small house with their father. Their parents were divorced.

Roseann felt that her father did not love her. He gave Doreen lots of special presents. But he hardly gave Roseann anything. When Doreen yelled at Roseann, their father always took Doreen's side.

A Father's Crime

Roseann's father often made her leave the house at night. He told her to go to a friend's house. Or he told her to just go outside.

One night Roseann came back early. She opened the door quietly. She heard her father and Doreen making noises in the bedroom. She had heard those noises when her father and mother had "private time." She had heard those noises on TV.

She knew they were the noises people made when they had intercourse.

She was very confused. The next day she asked Doreen what had happened. Doreen told her to shut up and mind her own business.

Another time Roseann came into the house and saw Doreen naked in her father's bedroom. Her father had gone out. When Roseann came into the bedroom, Doreen started to cry. Roseann put her arm around her older sister. She asked what was wrong.

Doreen said, "Daddy did something dirty to me." Roseann was scared. "I don't understand," she said. Then Doreen told Roseann about incest.

What Is Incest?

Incest means having sexual activity with someone who is related to you. This can be a family member who lives in your house, like a father or sister. Or it can be a relative who does not live with you, like your cousin or grandfather.

Any sexual activity between a child and another family member can be called incest. Sexual intercourse does not have to happen. If a family member touches private parts of your body, this is considered incest. If a family member makes you look at or touch his or her naked body, this is also incest. When a family member forces you to watch or be part of *pornographic* pictures, this is incest, too.

He grabbed her and threw her onto the couch...
He said he would hit her.
But she kept yelling for help.

What Types of People Commit Incest?

Incest can happen in rich or poor families. It can happen in homes where parents are living together or where they're divorced. Although the abuser is often male—a father, brother, uncle, grandfather—this is not always true. Sometimes the abuser is a female. The type of incest that is the most difficult for children to recover from is committed by a parent.

Incest happens most often in homes where the abuser was an incest victim as a child. Incestuous families may prefer to keep to themselves. They don't want their behavior to be discovered by outsiders.

Many abusers have trouble getting along with people their own age. They have few friends. They may try to keep their victims from having friends, too, so no one learns about the incest.

When an abuser is discovered, he or she may make excuses or try to blame someone else. For example, a father might claim that it is better for him to have sex with his daughter than to go outside the family to another woman. An older sister might say that she and her little brother were just "playing doctor." A lonely mother might turn to her son for sex if her husband ran out on the family. But the truth is, there is no excuse for incest. Only the abuser is to blame.

Roseann Becomes the Victim

When Doreen told Roseann she was moving out, Roseann began crying. "Watch out or he'll do it to you," Doreen said. She hugged her little sister. After Doreen moved out, Roseann was afraid of her father. At night she heard him walking around the house. When he wanted her to stay home, she found excuses to go out.

One night Roseann was reading. Her father was drinking beer. He asked her to dance. Roseann was afraid. She said okay. Her father started to rub her in a sexual way. When the music stopped, he held her tight.

"Come on," he told her. He wanted her to go to his bedroom. "I'll show you what your sister liked," he said. Roseann screamed and hit her father with her fists. When he let go she ran out of the house.

Roseann went to her aunt's house. She told her aunt what happened. Her aunt didn't believe Roseann and got angry. Then she called her father. Her father took her back home. He told her if she told anyone again, he would kill her.

Several weeks later Roseann's father was drunk. He grabbed her and threw her onto a couch. He tore her clothes. She started to scream again. He said he would hit her. But she kept yelling for help.

A neighbor called the police. When the police came, Roseann's father went to the door. He told the police everything was all right. But Roseann told the police what had happened. She showed them her torn clothes. They put handcuffs on her father and took him to jail. Later Roseann talked to a police officer who works with children. She told the police officer that her father had intercourse with her sister Doreen. The police officer saw that Roseann understood this was incest. Doreen also talked to the police officer.

The police officer called Roseann's aunt. She helped Roseann's aunt understand what had happened. Roseann went to live with her aunt.

Being a Victim of Incest

Incest is one of the worst forms of sexual abuse because it destroys a family's trust in each other. Victims of incest may get angry at other family members for not protecting them. Roseann may have been angry at Doreen because she left her alone with their father. Both daughters might have been angry at their mother for leaving and not protecting them from incest.

Remembering the Rules

The most important rule in this story is Rule #6, Keep Telling People About Sexual Abuse Until Someone Listens.

Sometimes, adults don't believe children who talk about sexual abuse. Sometimes they even get angry, like Roseann's aunt. It is very hard for an adult to believe someone in their family could commit sexual abuse.

Roseann didn't tell anyone else because she was scared. Her father said he would kill her. But the next time he abused her, she screamed so much a neighbor called the police. Even though the police asked her a lot of questions, she made them believe her. Incest is a crime. So Roseann's father was arrested.

For victims of incest, Rules #6 and #7 are even harder to follow because a family member is involved. Many children worry that if they report incest, they will be taken away from their homes. Others fear that if they tell, they will send a family member to jail. Often the abusers threaten children with terrible punishments if they talk. But remember, even if the person abusing you is your own father or mother, Keep Talking Until Someone Listens. What Happens to a Sexual Abuser is Never Your Fault.

Chapter 8

The Crime of Rape

When Debra was sexually abused by her grandfather, she told her teacher, Mrs. Markle. Then, Mrs. Markle called the child protection service. She also called Debra's mom. Debra's mom was mad that Debra hadn't told her about the abuse. But her mom knew that Debra was afraid Grandpa would have to leave.

Rosa's Story

Debra was lucky because her mom knew what to do. Rosa is a girl who was not so lucky.

When Rosa was 11, her father died of a heart attack. She lived with her mother and little six-year old brother, Juanito. A young friend of Rosa's father named Julio lived in her building.

Julio quit school when he was sixteen. Now, he did odd jobs, played cards with his friends and just hung out on the street.

A father has to listen to his child and try to understand what the child is feeling.

One day, when 11-year-old Rosa was coming home from school, Julio was rapping with his friends. He showed her a bracelet he had in his pocket and asked if she liked it. When she said yes, he gave it to her. He winked at his pals. The next day, he bought Rosa a soda. Then, a week later, she saw him again. He told her to follow him. He smiled like he had a secret place he wanted to show her. She was scared, but a little excited too. She felt really grown up. She liked the attention she was getting from Julio. She thought something special might happen.

Julio led Rosa down to the basement of a nearby building. "You wanna be my girl?" he asked her.

Rosa didn't know what to say. She was nervous. So she just stared. Before she knew what was happening, Julio was holding her and rubbing up against her. Then he let go. "You like that?" he asked. "I bet you never felt a man."

Rosa turned and wanted to run. But Julio jumped in front of her. He was still smiling. "Come on," he said. "We're going to have some fun." Then he pushed her into a small room with a mattress on the floor.

Rosa tried to resist. But Julio was too strong. He forced her to have sex. Then, he put a dollar in her pocket. He said that if she told anyone, he would kill her little brother. She was very frightened for Juanito's safety. He was so helpless!

Rosa was also afraid that her mother would find out what happened. She had told her that girls who had sex before they were married went to hell.

Julio took Rosa to the basement many times after that. If she didn't fight and just let him do what he wanted, he promised not to hurt Juanito. She hated his smell and felt awful when it was over, down in her stomach. But she was scared to tell anyone.

One day, Mrs. Sanchez saw Julio and Rosa in the basement. She guessed what was going on and called Rosa's Mom.

Mom: (on the phone) I can't believe this. You sure it was her?

Rosa: What's wrong Mom?

Mom: That was Mrs. Sanchez. She told me what you're doing with that guy Julio. God is going to punish you for this.

Rosa: (scared) What are you talking about? I didn't do anything.

Mom: You lie to me? I'll teach you to lie, you little puta! How much did he pay you?

Now, Rosa was confused. She had taken money. But only because Julio made her. Then, Rosa's mom slapped her. She started to cry.

Rosa: (crying) Mom, he hurt me and said he would kill Juanito. I couldn't stop him. I don't like him. I hate what he does. Help me, Mom. I'm so scared. I don't know what to do.

Mom: How could he make you do that if you don't want to? What do you think will happen now? No one will want you. You'll never get married. Mrs. Sanchez will tell everyone in the neighborhood. Everyone will

The sexual abuser often feels alone and separated from the people around him.

laugh at me. I'm going to find Julio and scratch his eyes out and then I'll deal with you.

Rosa's mother ran out the door. Rosa was scared about what she might do. She just sat and cried.

The next day, Rosa heard what happened. Her mom and Julio got into a violent argument and the police had to be called to break it up. They had to go to the police station. When Rosa's mom finally got home she was afraid to talk about what had happened. Rosa wanted to run away from home.

Later that summer, Rosa's aunt came to visit from Puerto Rico. When she heard what happened, she called Rosa aside.

"Rosa," she said, "you were raped." Rosa had heard the word before and knew rape was a terrible thing. But she had not thought this was what happened to her. She thought rape was only by strangers.

"When I was a girl, I was raped too," said Rosa's aunt. "Whenever someone makes you have sex against your will, that is rape," she said. "You weren't bad. What Julio did was a terrible crime and he should be punished. You feel guilty because you took money and because your mother got into trouble with the police. But you took money because you were scared and didn't know what to do.

"This Julio has a serious problem," Rosa's aunt explained. "You made a mistake and got tricked. But adults are stronger and bigger than kids. That's why kids need help when adults force them to do something they don't want to do. Lots of kids make mistakes worse than the one you made."

Rosa asked her aunt, "What should I do now?"
"We're going to call the police. Then you and I are going to explain to them what happened. Then I will talk to your mother.
Rosa was worried. "What will they do to Julio?"

"They'll punish him and then they'll get him help so he doesn't trick or hurt any more girls. You know, Rosa, if he did this to you, he probably did it to other girls before. We're going to stop him. You and me. Okay?"

Rosa wasn't sure, but she said okay.

What Is Rape?

Julio forced Rosa to have sex against her will. This form of sexual abuse is called rape. When we think of rape we think of strangers. Rosa knew Julio. Most rapes are committed by people who know their victim.

Remembering the Rules

Remember Rule #1, Your Body Belongs to You. No one has the right to make you have sex when you don't want it. Rape is a very serious crime.

When Rosa told her mother about her sexual abuse, she could only think about herself and her family's pride. Her first thought was how to hurt Julio, not how to protect and help Rosa.

What should Rosa's mother have done?

First, she could have told her about rape. Then, she could have explained Rule #2, Abuse is Never Your Fault. This would have been very hard for her to do. Rosa's mother loves her. So she got mad when Rosa was hurt. But even if she took money, Julio was the one

Teenagers want to be liked by adults. But no one has to allow unwanted touching.

who was wrong, not Rosa. After she got mad, she should have listened to Rosa more closely. She should have tried to figure out what she was feeling.

What Happens to an Abuser Is Never Your Fault

The day after Rosa talked to the police, everyone at school was talking about her and Julio. Julio's sister told Rosa she would get her after school. Julio's friends made fun of Rosa.

But then Laura Sanchez came up to Rosa. Laura was the daughter of the woman who had seen Rosa and Julio in the basement. Laura told Rosa that Julio had done the same thing to her. The two girls held each other and cried. Then, Laura told the police everything.

Julio went on trial. At the trial Rosa and Laura told their stories. Rosa's aunt came to court too. So did a police woman who works with victims of rape and sexual abuse.

Julio was sent to jail. In jail he got therapy. Each week, he went to a group with other men who had abused or raped girls. Rosa graduated from high school and was working at a store in the neighborhood. Julio got out of jail after two years and moved back home. But he never bothered Rosa, Laura or any other girls in the neighborhood. Today, Rosa and Laura are still friends.

Boys Can Be Raped, Too

Usually we think of rape victims as girls. But one out of every six boys in the United States is raped or sexually abused every year. Often, the victims are boys without fathers living at home. Since nearly half of all African-American homes have no fathers, the male children are at special risk.

What kind of people rape boys? Often it's men who were sexually abused themselves. Child rapists are *pedophiles*. They are usually *heterosexual* (having sexual feelings toward people of the opposite sex), not homosexual. When these men have sex with someone their own age, they prefer women, not men.

Men who rape boys rarely get violent. But the abuse may still hurt, both physically and mentally. Chuck was six years old when he was first raped by his cousin. "He pulled my pajama bottoms down and forced his way into my anus with his penis. The skin broke and I began to bleed." Chuck was raped many times by his cousin, but he didn't tell anyone for 15 years. During that time, he suffered just as much mentally as he did physically.

If Chuck had known Rule #5, Sexual Abuse Does Not Stop By Itself, he might have told someone sooner. Many boys keep "their secret" to themselves because their abusers threaten them if they tell. Even those who do talk are not always believed. They must remember Rule #6, Keep Talking Until Someone Listens. "The most powerful thing a parent or relative can do," says one psychologist, "is to believe the child."

Chapter 9

How You Can Help Stop Sexual Abuse

Another kind of sexual abuse that is growing more common is the problem of kids molesting other kids. Some of the molesters are as young as three or four. "It's too frightening for most people to believe," says Sandra Ballester, who is head of a program to help treat young child molesters.

Most of these abusers have one thing in common. Like Sam (who was abused by Billy in Chapter 6), they have been victims of sexual abuse themselves. They do to other children what was done to them. Very often these children come from homes where parents are separated. One or both parents may be alcoholic or drug addicted. In homes like this, the children are usually neglected.

They make easy targets for sexual abuse. And once
they become victims, they're very likely to turn
into abusers themselves.

What can be done to stop the problems? One of
the most important steps that any of us can take is
to remember Rule #6: Keep Telling People You
Trust Until Someone Listens. If you or someone
you know has been abused, don't be afraid to talk
about it!

At Sandra Ballester's center, "children are told
that they *themselves* are not evil. It is their
molesting behavior that is a monster." *Therapists*
(child workers) use puppets to act the part of the
monster in little plays. When children see how
these monsters behave, it often helps them correct
their own behavior. After the monster has
performed its horrible act, a therapist might ask
one of the children, "Remember how you felt when
this happened to you? How do you think other
children feel when you do this to them?"

But the real problem, says another therapist from
Michigan, "is that parents often refuse to believe
what their children have done." This is why it is so
important to keep talking about abuse you see until
someone listens to you. There is help for sexual
abusers. There is help for children who are
victims. But we will never stop this horrible cycle
of abuse as long as we keep sexual abuse a secret.

Glossary —*Explaining New Words*

abuser   Someone you know and trust who tries to hurt you sexually.

genitals   These are sexual organs. Examples of genitals are a boy's penis and a girl's vagina.

heterosexual   Having sexual feelings toward people of the opposite sex.

homosexual   Having sexual feelings toward people of the same sex.

incest   Sexual activity between two people who are closely related.

intercourse   When the male penis is placed inside the vagina of a female.

molester   A stranger or someone you barely know who tries to hurt you sexually.

pedophile   An adult who enjoys sexual activity with children.

pornography   Pictures, films, or stories that clearly show sexual activity for the purpose of arousing sexual desire.

privacy   The right to be left alone.

psychologist   A doctor who studies the mind and helps to treat mental problems.

rape   When one person forces another person to have sexual relations.

survivor   Someone who was hurt or abused in the past.

therapist   A person trained to help treat mental or physical problems.

victim   Someone who is being hurt or abused.

Where to Go for Help

When you or someone you know has a problem with sexual abuse, there are many places you can go for help outside of your family. Librarians, teachers, social workers, doctors, counselors, religious leaders, or police officers can help you find people in your area that will be able to help. If you're afraid to tell someone you know, or if you can't find help nearby, try calling one of the numbers below.

The Clearinghouse on Child Abuse & Neglect Information: 1-800-394-3366. In the Washington DC area, call 1-703-385-7565.
Childhelp USA: 1-800-4-A-CHILD
Child Protection Program Foundation: 1-214-790-0300
National Committee For Prevention of Child Abuse: 1-312-663-3520

For Further Reading

Benedict, Helen. *Safe, Strong, & Streetwise.* Boston: Little, Brown and Company, 1987, 196 pages. Discusses sexual safety at home, on the street, on dates, on the job, and more.

Farrell, Mary H.J. "Oprah's Crusade." *People*, December 2, 1991, pages 68-69. Article on Oprah Winfrey's efforts to aid victims of child sexual abuse.

Gelman, David. "When Kids Molest Kids." *Newsweek*, March 30, 1992, pages 68-70. Psychologists' efforts to understand and treat a younger group of sex offenders.

Gite, Lloyd. "When Boys Are Raped." *Essence*, November 1991, pages 61-62 + . Article discusses boys as victims of sexual abuse.

Miller, Deborah A. and Kelly, Pat. *Coping With Incest*. New York: The Rosen Publishing Group, 1992, 156 pages. Talks about society's great secret in a straightforward way.

Index

About the Author
Evan Stark is a well-known sociologist, educator, and therapist as well as
a popular lecturer on women's and children's health issues. Dr. Stark was
the Henry Rutgers Fellow at Rutgers University, an associate at the Insti-
tution for Social and Policy Studies at Yale University, and a Fulbright
Fellow at the University of Essex. He is the author of many publications
in the field of family relations and is the father of four children.

Acknowledgments and Photo Credits

P. 20, Blackbirch Graphics, Inc.; all other photos, Stuart Rabinowitz.

Design/Production: Blackbirch Graphics, Inc.
Cover Photograph: Stuart Rabinowitz